BEHIND THE BEGATS

Conversations for
Thanksgiving and Advent

William M. Aber

BEHIND THE BEGATS

PRINTED IN U.S.A.

To Ted and Jean Aber,
who begat me.

TABLE OF CONTENTS

INTRODUCTION

None of us who grew up with the King James Version of the Bible could fail to be delighted when we first saw the musical *Porgy and Bess* and heard Cab Calloway sing, "The Begats." For there was a spoof, in a way that we had never ourselves dared to enunciate, of the one portion of Scripture that had always appeared to be less than inspiring when we heard it read. It had, in fact, been absolutely boring when ploughed through by a minister as part of the morning Scripture lesson!

The theme of "The Begats" was taken from the first chapter of Matthew's Gospel where the ancestral roots of Jesus were listed in a genealogical table that went on and on for sixteen verses saying simply that "Abram begat Isaac; Isaac begat Jacob; Jacob begat Judas . . ." and so on down to Joseph, the husband of Mary. Newer translations of the Bible have replaced "begat" with "was the father of" which renders the passage more readily understandable, less musical, but equally boring!

Boring, that is, until we take the time to look at those names on the list of Jesus' ancestors. Then we discover not only some surprises, but also some jumping off places for serious discussion of various facets of the Christian faith. It is, for example, surprising to an age in which women were not only unliberated, but characterized in one of God's commandments as chattel, on a par with a neighbor's house, servants, or cattle, to discover that women were considered important enough to be named along with men in that particular genealogy. We would expect to find David the king on that list; it is somewhat astounding to come upon Rahab the prostitute as well. Abraham, the patriarch of the Jews, obviously belongs; Ruth the Moabitess is a bit of a surprise. And so it goes.

The season of Advent, and also Thanksgiving, is a time for looking toward the Incarnation, the coming of God to earth in Jesus the Christ. Perhaps we can best prepare ourselves to consider that coming as we look at a few of those who came before. The sermons which follow are dialogues about some of the names on the list of Jesus' ancestors. As the discussions go on, it becomes evident that a number of major theological themes are suggested by the lives and activities of those who formed the heritage of Jesus' earthly family.

These dialogue sermons could be used as the beginning of a Bible study group, but they would also be appropriate for delivery by pastors, or laypersons, as a part of the regular worship service on Sunday morning. Behind the begats are some of the cornerstones of our faith.

A DIALOGUE FOR THANKSGIVING
GOD'S PILGRIM PEOPLE
ABRAHAM

FIRST SPEAKER (1): When you get right down to it, Thanksgiving is a rather strange holiday for our nation to celebrate in these times.

SECOND SPEAKER [2]: Why do you say that? Surely you're not so cynical as to say there's no reason for us to give thanks?

1: Of course not! I'm as thankful as anyone for all that we have, and all that we are. I'm just not sure what Thanksgiving Day is all about.

2: What do you mean?

1: Well, it obviously began as a harvest festival, but we're no longer a nation of farmers.

2: That may be, but we still produce a lot of food.

1: Yes we do, but disposal of farm surplusses continues to be a pressing problem for us. And our collective cholestoral count in the face of hunger in the rest of the world makes me feel a bit guilty about celebrating our own abundance.

2: Well, I see what you mean, but there is biblical precedent for giving thanks . . .

1: That's right, and that's another strange thing. Thanksgiving is a religious holiday proclaimed by the state, yet our prevailing philosophy holds that the state should not invade the realm of the sacred. Actually, Thanksgiving even became a political football back in 1939 when President Roosevelt changed the date from the fourth Thursday in November to the third one. We ended up with a "Republican Thanksgiving" and a "Democratic Thanksgiving" some places that year!

2: *I'd forgotten about that one. We may not have political football now, but we have lots of other football on Thanksgiving . . . In fact, ask people what they associate with the day and they'll probably say football games.*

1: Or turkeys.

2: *Right. Or maybe pilgrims.*

1: Hey, I think you've got it.

2: *What do you mean?*

1: "Pilgrims!" That's what Thanksgiving's all about, after all.

2: *Well, sure. Every school child knows that. We know all about that first Thanksgiving in New England . . .*

1: No, no. I don't mean that kind of pilgrim, or at least — not specifically.

2: *You don't? I don't understand.*

1: When I say "pilgrim," I'm not talking about the people we see in pictures this season — men wearing black knickers along with big hats with belt buckles on them, and women wearing bonnets and long gray dresses.

2: *I'm not sure you describe them accurately, but those are the pilgrims most of us associate with Thanksgiving, aren't they?*

1: I suppose so. But, I wonder if there aren't some others that are even more appropriate. What does the dictionary say about pilgrims?

2: *Well, one definition is:*
   "One of the 102 separatists from the church of England who landed from the Mayflower at Plymouth Colony, the first settlement in New England in 1620."

1: Right. But what else does it say?

2: *This particular dictionary also describes a pilgrim as "a wanderer, a wayfarer, or one who travels to some holy place."*

1: That's it!

2: *I'm still not sure that I follow you.*

1: Thanksgiving is a time for acknowledging our pilgrim status. It's a time for giving thanks to God that we are contemporary pilgrims; we are, in fact, God's pilgrim people.

2: *I'm afraid that you'll have to spell that out a little more for me. Maybe then I can catch the drift.*

1: In the Book of Hebrews, the Old Testament patriarchs or leaders are called "strangers and pilgrims on earth."

2: *I think I know that passage, although I thought it said "exiles," rather than "pilgrims."*

1: Oh, some of the newer translations use "exiles" or "aliens," but the meaning is clear. The early leaders saw themselves as pilgrims — that is — as *wanderers for God.* They were seeking a holy place, and finally came to realize that the land on which they settled was only a temporary dwelling place — a way station on the way to a promised land, to a new country, to a new beginning.

2: *And you're saying that we should be seeking something, too? That we're only pilgrims on this earth?*

1: Exactly! We're seeking for something more — a new kind of world where people can love one another, where they can be themselves, where nations are reconciled and individuals accepted. We're God's pilgrim people, on the road to a new place.

2: *So you're talking about heaven, then?*

1: Not really, although I suppose most folks tend to interpret that passage in Hebrews in that fashion. I'm saying that we're called by God to seek a better world here and now, to move toward a kind of existence where his will is known and his love is made manifest. That's what it means to be God's pilgrim.

2: *That's a big order! I've sure got no idea how to get to that new world.*

1: Maybe you don't have to! "Know how to get there," that is.

2: *What do you mean?*

1: Well, Abraham was certainly the prototype pilgrim in the Bible. And we read that "he went out, not knowing where he was to go . . ."

2: *You're right about him, but I'm sure no Abraham! So quotations like that don't help very much.*

1: You may be more like Abraham than you think. And this season is a time for giving thanks for it.

2: *I'm not following you yet, but keep talking.*

1: Let's begin by admitting that Thanksgiving, first of all, is *a time for trusting God.* Trust is what Abraham had, and any pilgrim must have to participate in a pilgrimage.

2: *Why is Thanksgiving so much a time for trust?*

1: We already said that it's a holiday that — for better or for worse — seems to center around food.

2: *That's for sure!*

1: If there's one thing that should make us perfectly aware of our own limitations it's the fact we can't produce our own food all alone.

2: *You can say that again! It's all I can do to grow grass. My wife manages to raise a few tomatoes, but I wouldn't want to have to live off the land by my own efforts. I'd starve.*

1: So would I. Virtually everything on our table is the result of someone else's efforts. But, even more than that, it's a result of God's providence. Food is a part of creation; and it's the best symbol we have of our dependence upon God. Thanksgiving's emphasis on food is one thing that ought to focus our attention upon God and our need to trust him. He's created a world for us. To accept that world is to trust God . . . and to enjoy.

2: *I guess I'd agree with that. I enjoy life . . . and I certainly enjoy eating. I suppose everybody does.*

1: I'm not so sure! I read once that Sir Walter Scott's father was a strict disciplinarian. When young Walter was enjoying soup at one meal, with perhaps excessive smacking of lips and slurping of broth, the father picked up the bowl and threw it on the floor. "Food is meant to eat," he is supposed to have exclaimed, "not to enjoy!"

2: *Wow! He must have missed a great deal of fun in life.*

1: Right. He didn't realize that we were created for joy. God's creation is good. Rejoicing in it, and giving thanks for it, is an expression of trust in God. To be thankful and to be trusting of God is to begin to be God's pilgrim people.

2: *I'm sure you're right. But, even as I say that, I realize that it's difficult for me fully to enjoy the creation. I can't be filled with joy when I know there is so much suffering in the world. I feel guilty taking a second helping of turkey on Thanksgiving Day when I know that people are starving to death in other parts of the world.*

1: As a matter of fact, people much closer to you than that may be starving. And it's good that you feel some sensitivity to their needs. That, too, is part of Thanksgiving. It is *a time to seek to do God's will.* To be aware of one's own blessings is, for the Christian, also to be moved to share those blessings with others.

2: *But sharing is so difficult! The problems of hunger are so complex that I don't know where to begin. I don't have all the answers.*

1: Nobody does. In the play *1776* one character says to another, "All questions are easy when someone else has to answer them." Well, we have to do the answering about world hunger . . . and that's hard.

2: *I remember a prayer/poem by Michel Quoist where he says how hard it is to feed the world, how he would rather say regular prayers, or give to charity, or whatever, but — as he ends the poem — "apparently that isn't enough . . . if one day You can say to me, 'I was hungry!' "*

1: He's right. Our call is to respond to human need, and the New Testament makes it quite clear that when anyone is hungry, Christ himself is in that hunger.

2: *So how do we respond?*

1: We look around, and use our own God-given minds to respond as best we can. Perhaps it's legislatively, working to change the food policy of our nation. Perhaps its seeing that day care, school lunch programs, meals for the elderly, and other programs are in operation where you live. Perhaps it's setting aside two cents per person at each meal to put in your own two cents worth through the church's hunger program. Perhaps it's more . . . but you get the picture by now.

2: *O.K., I act as best I can, realizing that God can and does work through me.*

1: Right. To be a pilgrim means to move out in faith — faith that there is something toward which we are called to move, and faith that God will enable us to move for some purpose.

2: *God uses me ... I like that! But I'm also a bit uncertain about it. Because, as I said earlier, I'm no Abraham. I'm not really sure that I'm the kind of person God wants for a pilgrim.*

1: That's interesting. What do you think Abraham was like?

2: *Well, I don't exactly know — but he was a towering figure in the Old Testament, the first of the patriarchs. He's called a man of faith; he served God without question. He's certainly what I'd call a saint.*

1: He probably was a saint, in the New Testament sense of that word. But so are you!

2: *What?*

1: A saint is simply any person who is called to be a part of God's people. You're called to sainthood just as as much as Abraham. Furthermore, Abraham was certainly less than perfect; and, as a man of faith, he was often less than faithful.

2: *Really?*

1: Sure! Read those stories about Abraham in Genesis again. You'll discover that, on at least two occasions during his pilgrimage, Abraham passed off his wife as his sister — in effect sending her off to a harem — just to save his own neck!

2: *Wow! If I'd read that, I must have forgotten it. Abraham was human after all.*

1: Of course. And maybe that's the final message about Thanksgiving: God calls human beings — even sinners — to be his pilgrims.

2: *Well, that is the Christian message, all right. Although I'm not quite sure that I see how it's a particular message of Thanksgiving Day.*

1: How do you picture a Thanksgiving dinner?

2: *Oh, as a time of joy — the whole family gathered around the table, singing, eating, talking, enjoying one another.*

1: I don't want to be cynical, but are all your Thanksgiving dinners really like that?

2: *Hmm. Well, maybe that is a bit idealized . . . like a Norman Rockwell painting. I guess, if I'm honest, I remember the carving of turkey taking forever when I was younger . . . and also how bored I was with the adult conversation! And there was usually an argument about who got the drumsticks!*

1: Exactly. Generation gaps are not automatically plugged just because a turkey sits in the middle of the table; tensions, frustrations, and annoyances don't go away just because some long unseen aunts and uncles have arrived for a holiday meal.

2: *As a matter of fact, there were probably some tensions at that first Thanksgiving in Massachusetts when those long-faced Puritans sat down with their potential enemies, with the question of survival never far from their minds.*

1: Right! But the point is, in the midst of our own less than perfect relationships, God is present. He comes to us, offering us the bounties of Creation, even though we are sinners.

2: *Hey, I like that! God comes to us in the midst of our sin ... and even calls us to follow him as we are.*

1: You've got it! Like Abraham, we're called to be pilgrims. Like him, we often falter and stumble, and do things that are utterly, unequivocally wrong. But through it all, God is with us.

2: *And I guess there's even more to it, isn't there?*

1: Right. God changes us. You may remember in reading about Abraham that growth occurred. In fact, he becomes not only magnanimous to a somewhat undeserving nephew, he actually becomes an intercessor for a people. As he traveled in faith and trust, God made him into a new person.

2: *And that's the real reason for giving thanks? Because we can be new?*

1: That's the real reason for our creation. So that we might respond to God, become his pilgrim people, and let his forgiving spirit create newness of life in us all.

2: *To be God's pilgrim people, then, is to be open to God's forgiveness?*

1: That's it. God calls us to be pilgrims, not because we're good — but because we need to be changed, because we need to become new people ...

2: *... and he makes us new in Jesus Christ! That's what you've been aiming at all along. I can see that now.*

1: Yes, Jesus Christ is at the center of Thanksgiving. Through his death and resurrection, forgiveness is made possible and available. Through him, God's pilgrim people become God's redeemed.

2: *You know, I really love the great Thanksgiving hymns,* Come Ye Thankful People Come *and* Now Thank We All Our God. *But I just thought of a hymn that may sum up everything that we've been saying about Thanksgiving.*

1: Which one is that?

2: *He Who Would Valiant Be.*

1: It's about God's pilgrim people, isn't it?

2: *Right, and I can sing it with confidence now, since I realize that God has called even me to be one of his pilgrims. Remember the last verse:*
   Since, Lord, Thou dost defend us with Thy Spirit,
   We know we at the end shall life inherit.
   Then, fancies, flee away! I'll fear not what men say,
   I'll labor night and day to be a pilgrim.

1: Amen.

A DIALOGUE FOR
THE FIRST SUNDAY IN ADVENT
GOD'S HERITAGE
ISAAC

FIRST READER (1): I was sure confused when I heard the music this morning. It sounded as though we were still celebrating Thanksgiving.

SECOND READER (2): It did, didn't it? We sang Watchman, Tell Us of the Night *using the same tune that we also use for* Come, Ye Thankful People, Come. *That's appropriate, though; it seems to make Thanksgiving blend into Advent almost without effort.*

1: I suppose it does, but Advent should be much more than giving thanks. It's supposed to be a time for looking ahead, a season of preparation for Christmas.

2: *Of course, but what better way to prepare than to continue to cultivate an attitude of thankfulness? If we feel gratitude toward God for his creation, we're more apt to offer our supreme thanks for God's supreme gift — Christ himself. That's why I like the Thanksgiving-Advent connection.*

1: That does make sense, all right, but I still have a bit of confusion about the direction these conversations seem to be leading.

2: *How so?*

1: Well, Advent is indeed a time of expectation, of looking toward the "long expected Jesus." It's a season of preparation, of noting the signs of promise.

2: *Right. So what's the problem?*

1: Well, it seems to me that we're looking in the wrong direction. Oh, I guess that we're preparing for Christmas, but we seem to be going about it backwards. Instead of looking toward Jesus, we're looking back to his ancestors. We discussed Abraham last week, and now we're going to look at Isaac. I don't see how reviewing the past helps us very much in the present. Knowing about the patriarchs doesn't assist me in comprehending the Incarnation.

2: *Don't be too sure. You may find that you're confronted by Jesus in strange places, even in a look at his genealogy! Anyway, there are all kinds of ways to observe Advent. In Normandy, farmers still employ children to run through their fields with lighted torches, setting fires to little bundles of straw. That's supposed to drive out the vermin so that the baby Jesus might have a clean bed. Would you opt for that?*

1: I surely never heard of that custom. I'll admit that any kind of Bible study would be more helpful than some supersititon about lighting fires in the fields . . .

2: *Don't misunderstand me; I'm not making light of that custom. As a symbol, it's probably every bit as meaningful to the participants as our Advent wreaths are to us. [And our wreaths involve the lighting of candles, so they're not so different at that!] What I'm suggesting is that there is a wide variety of ways to prepare for Christmas, and there may well be some surprising confrontations with Jesus Christ no matter which direction we take.*

1: O.K., let's take another look at Jesus' earthly roots and see if you're right. I'm not sure, though, that Isaac will prove very helpful. Abraham was at least a towering figure — the father of the Jewish nation, in fact. All I can remember about his son Isaac is something about digging out his father's wells.

2: *"He digged again the wells his father digged." That's the way the King James Version of the Bible put it, and it may well sum him up. He was a conservative. He looked back at the old ways. And in so doing, oddly enough, he may help us in our Advent preparation.*

1: If so, I'll be surprised! How can a man like Isaac tell us anything? He had no original thoughts that I can see — not even as to the whereabouts of new water wells! He certainly never did any noteworthy things. In fact he seems to play a passive role every time he appears in the Bible. As a boy he is almost sacrificed by his father; as an old man he is deceived by his youngest son. He doesn't capture our imaginations ever by anything that he says or does.

2: *You forgot to mention that of all the patriarchs, he was the only one with just one wife. That, too, may mark him as not very adventurous!*

1: Well, it at least bears out the fact of his conservatism. And my point is still the same: What can he tell us about Christmas?

2· *I'm surprised that you haven't guessed. Even if Christmas isn't as old as we once thought — the 4th century being the earliest that we have any record of a December twenty-fifth celebration for Christ's nativity — it is certainly a very old holiday. And maybe our preparation for Christmas this year should begin with the realization that there is a value in that which is old.*

1: Well, that's a different twist, anyhow. Most of the merchants these days are doing their best to induce us to buy things that are new.

2: *Are they ever! Part of today's merchandising seems to aim to make us dissatisfied with the old — to have us feel that anything produced before this split second is about as obsolete as if it were left over from Noah's Ark!*

1: And I suppose that goes for ideas, too?

2: *Of course! These days most old ideas and ideals are either patronized as quaint anachronisms or brushed aside as useless relics of the past.*

1: But Isaac saw things differently?

2: *Yes. He looked backwards to some old ideals, virtues, and concepts, and he simply took them as his own.*

1: What sort of ideals did he appropriate for his life?

2: *Well,* family love and solidarity, *for one. I'm not sure what kind of model he had in Abraham and Sarah. Something must have moved him, though, for he remained a family man all his life. He loved his parents, his wife, and his sons. There are some tender scenes in Genesis portraying that love. In an age where the family unit was often disrupted, where monogamy was the exception rather than the rule, he found a real value in hearth and home.*

1: I guess that is an appropriate value for us, at that. Particularly at Christmas.

2: *Right you are. It's significant, I think, that Christmas began in a family event . . . that is, the birth of a child. At the very lowest level of its importance, the incarnation of God in Jesus Christ is an indication of the sanctity of the family. God used a family as his vehicle for becoming part of his creation. Certainly one way to cultivate the Christmas spirit is to strengthen the family as a vital part of society.*

1: I can't agrue with that, of course. (Who wants to speak against motherhood!) There does seem to be real reason for looking back and recapturing the notion that the family unit is of great importance, and for working to let love be real within all of our families. But the fact of the matter is that there are a great many persons in our society who aren't a part of what we think of as the typical family. There are single persons, widows and widowers, divorced persons, as well as people with what we euphemistically call alternative life styles. What can a nostalgic look at the old fashioned family bring but loneliness or guilt? What kind of word does Isaac have for them?

2: *Maybe his word for them is* peace!

1: Peace! What does that mean? Everybody's for peace, of course. "Peace on earth" is certainly a watchword of the season. But how does it become more than a cliche? What does it really mean to any of us?

2: *If you look at Isaac's stories, you discover that he was a man of peace. Peace was an old virtue; and he made it his way of life. He did it through love. In a violent age, not unlike our own, love enabled him to walk in peaceful ways.*

1: How so?

2: *You may remember that when a rival band of herdsmen quarrelled with Isaac about the rights to a particular well, he didn't fight. He simply moved on and said, "God will make room for all of us." He foreshadowed, in that event, a man who would one day tell others to turn the other cheek when struck, and to return good for evil. Christmas may well be a time for eschewing violence of all kinds, the violence of TV and the violence of national policy.*

1: How on earth do we do that?

2: *We begin, at least, by making love the basis for our actions. And love means caring for others, accepting others, understanding others, and seeking to meet their needs. It means responding to the world in ways other than violence. It's a looking back to the old virtues of peace and love, and giving them priority in life.*

1: Like motherhood, peace and love are difficult to oppose! What else does Isaac tell us through his backward look?

2: *Well, he seems to point back to* worship *as a major influence for living.*

1: I'm afraid that most people would see worship as an old virtue, all right. They'd also see it as a rather old fashioned one that has very little relevance for day to day living.

2: *Perhaps. When I hear things like that, however, I'm reminded of a sermon illustration I once heard about a woman who was complaining about her pastor. He had been ineffective in a time of trouble: "He had nothing new to tell me to help me," she said, "just the same old business about Christ, the resurrection and*

the life; nothing different, just the same old thing."
And the minister who was preaching that sermon
said, "May she lose some of her taste for novelty
before she comes herself to face the same old thing."

1: So you're saying that worship can help us face the problems of life and death?

2: *Of course. It speaks to life's problems and its joys as well.*

1: How does Isaac involve himself in worship? He certainly lived before the days of the temple, or of formalized services of worship.

2: *Through his covenant with God. God made a covenant, or promise, to him whereby he said, "I am with you." That's really what worship is all about: a time for responding to a God who has promised to be with us, and to relate to us. For most of us, relationships with God need common worship at its center. Gathering with others for prayer and praise helps us to be open to God's revelation of himself.*

1: O.K., I'll agree with what you've said. Christmas is a season where the old virtues seem to have meaning, where heritage God has given us of family, peace, love, and worship seems clear. Is it not a time for new things as well?

2: *I don't want to downgrade newness. As a matter of fact, our call is to become new people. But it is well to remember that in an old collection of writings, we find a proclamation that the highest value of life is summed up not in the "latest thing," but in the Ancient of Days. In him, newness of life can become real.*

1: You're right . . . and I just thought of something else.

2: *What's that?*

1: Well, Isaac looked back at old virtues, but he had to make them his own.

2: *That's right. He dug out the wells his father dug before him. He had to work on them himself, even though they had been used years earlier.*

1: Just like any of those old ideals. We have to do more than reflect on them. We have to make them a part of our lives. A nostalgic remembrance of happy times with the family, or of a meaningful candlelight Christmas Eve service years ago does very little to affect our present existence. We need to cultivate our own sense of caring about others, inside and outside of the family. We need to participate in worship experiences. We need to make love the highest priority of our existence.

2: *You've got it! That's precisely what I've been trying to say. I'll admit, however, that it's not quite as easy to do those things as we might wish. Loving others, as well as loving God, is much easier said than done.*

1: I wonder, though, if the major message from Isaac doesn't speak to just that problem?

2: *Now it's my turn to ask what you mean!*

1: Well, if I were to ask you to name the one incident from Isaac's life that is the most memorable, what would you say?

2: *That's easy. I can never forget that scene when, as a small boy, Isaac is almost offered up by his father as a sacrifice to God.*

1: That's the one event I'd choose, too. I suspect that the most important thing about Isaac is that he almost became a sacrificial offering. That a ram was substituted for the boy at the last minute takes nothing away from the drama of the event: Abraham, in response to the command of God, demonstrates his willingness to offer up his son as a human sacrifice.

2: *Of course! I see where you're going! You're suggesting that ultimately it is the sacrifice of a son that brings meaning and power to all of life.*

1: Right! That sacrifice of the Son of God. I don't know if the Isaac story is meant to be some sort of preview of the sacrifice of Jesus Christ, but no Christian can look at that event and not see some faint glimmerings of Calvary. In any case, it is the sacrifice of Christ that gives us not only hope, but the power to live different kinds of lives.

2: *We get that power through the fact of forgiveness.*

1: Right, again! The cross of Christ is the demonstration of God's love and forgiveness for us all. Knowing and accepting that forgiveness fills us with new spirit, with new abilities, with new life.

2: *And Christmas really points to that, doesn't it? We focus our attention on the manger . . . but the birth of Christ should never be seen apart from his sacrificial death and resurrection.*

1: That sacrifice is God's ultimate gift, which makes Christmas — as we said when we began this sermon — a time for thanksgiving!

2: *So it is; thanksgiving for an old story, a story of forgiveness and love. And that love empowers us to take old virtues of peace and love and make them our own.*

1: So that we become new!

2: *Amen!*

A DIALOGUE FOR
THE SECOND SUNDAY IN ADVENT
GOD'S DREAMS
RAHAB

First Reader (1): This time, I have a feeling that you've really gone too far!

Second Reader (2): What do you mean?

1: Proposing a discussion about Rahab for this Advent series! I'm willing to concede that a discussion of Old Testament patriarchs may have some merit. After all, God did provide a covenant through them, and the new covenant in Jesus Christ may be more meaningful if we understand the older one. To talk about Abraham, Isaac, and Jacob is one thing . . .

2: But to talk about Rahab is something else again, right?

1: Right! I guess she is on the list as one of the ancestors of Jesus, but the fact of the matter is that she's nothing less than — well — a lady of the streets!

2: You don't have to be so delicate with that euphemism; The Bible quite bluntly, and quite frequently, refers to her as "Rahab the harlot!"

1: Well, there you are! What can that kind of a woman possibly have to do with the Christmas season? Why should we talk about her in Advent?

2: There are, I think, some pretty good reasons. You know her story, of course . . .

1: Certainly. Rahab lived in a home of sun-dried brick, presumably built over the two walls surrounding the city of Jericho. It was apparently located at a strategic point, with at least one window overlooking the outer wall. For that reason, Israelite spies coming to reconnoiter the city's defenses in preparation for siege found their way to her house. Rahab hid these spies from the city authorities, aided their escape over the city wall, and extracted a promise from them that if they returned and captured the city, she and her family would be saved.

2: *Didn't you forget something?*

1: Well, I suppose you mean the fact that she indicated some vague comprehension of the God of Israel in her conversation with the spies.

2: *As it happens, it was more than "vague;" she had a fairly good understanding of him. And the city was, indeed, conquered by the Israelites who kept their bargain and spared Rahab and her family.*

1: I suppose we owe Rahab a vote of thanks for helping the spies. But I'm still not very impressed. She's not only a harlot, but also a traitor to her own people. Hardly the type of person for our Christmas time consideration!

2: *I think I could debate that issue with you on the basis that Christmas marks the anniversary of God's coming to humankind to deal with precisely that kind of person. [And Rahab may differ from you and me only in degree, anyway!] But, I want us to think about Rahab, herself. I really think she has a message for us.*

1: If so, it surely eludes me. Aside from the fact, that is, that if God comes to us in Christ to rescue sinners, Rahab richly qualifies for that title.

2: *I'll avoid the obvious rejoinder about throwing the first stone and all that. Instead, let's fantasize a bit about Rahab. We don't have a great deal of biblical information about her, but we can make a few rather logical deductions as we look at her story.*

1: Such as?

2: *Such as the fact that she probably was a dreamer. Apparently she lived alone, yet when she spoke to the spies about what might happen when they attacked the city, her concern was for her family. She asked that her parents, her brothers, her sisters — all, presumably, living in the city — be saved. It was not only possible, but probable, that Rahab's chosen profession had cut her off from her family. They undoubtedly had disowned her. Nevertheless, Rahab still cared about them.*

1: I suppose that's true.

2: *And don't forget the bit about God. Rahab knows more than one might imagine about the God of Israel and his power and purpose. She speaks of him, however, as your God — never "my" God or "our" God. She's cut off from him, as well as from family.*

1: That's probably right, but what does it have to do with dreaming?

2: *I suppose that it's only poetic license on my part, but I tend to read into her words a certain wistfulness. There seems to be a longing for a family relationship that no longer exists, for an understanding of a God not really known to her, but obviously known to the enemies of her city.*

1: I suppose she might have dreamed a bit, at that — dreamed about her family and about God and about relationships that she must have felt would never amount to anything. As I recall the story, she made linen from flax, and dried the stalks of flax on her rooftop. Maybe she did go up there to escape from the drunken breath, the foul mouths, and the bought love of the rooms below. Perhaps, under the stars in the cool of the evening, alone on the rooftop, she dreamed of what it would be like to be loved again by her family, or what it would be like to be known by God.

2: *Now who's got the poetic license? Anyway, that's the kind of scene that I picture. And dreaming, certainly, is a part of Christmas for all of us.*

1: Yes, it is. Dreams seem to go with Christmas, whether they are of sugar plums, or of white Christmases, or of family reunions.

2: *But, dreams are even more a part of Christmas than that. Remember the dreams at the first Christmas?*

1: Dreams? Oh, you mean the ones Joseph had?

2: *Right! God spoke to him in a dream, telling him that Mary was with child by the Holy Spirit, and that the child should be called Jesus for he would save his people from their sins.*

1: I guess you could say, then, that Christmas actually began with a dream. But what, if anything, is the connection with Rahab and her dreams?

2: *Maybe it's the fact that — as was the case with Joseph — God was the source of her dreaming.*

1: How do you figure that?

2: *Well, I'm not sure that I can prove it. But as I read Scripture, it seems obvious that God quite often reveals himself in dreams. The yearnings of Rahab seem to be precisely the kinds of dreams that God might produce.*

1: Why do you say that?

2: *Because God's will for us, as I understand it, is for love to be real, and for a relationship with him to be real. And the message of the Bible is that God himself takes the initiative, that he makes the first move to enable that love and that relationship to become a reality.*

1: So Rahab's dreams, and some of our own dreams for that matter, are really God's dreams?

2: *I think so. Rahab dreamed, and so do we, because God has already begun to break through. He gives us the dream, the yearning, the wistfulness, in order that we might be ready to receive his love.*

1: Well, it's a neat idea, anyhow. Is there anything else about the Rahab story that speaks to this season? I might have been too hasty in writing her off so soon.

2: *I think there are a couple of other things that we might discover in the story if we look for them. Rahab, you'll remember, made a venture. That is, she hid the Israelite spies and helped them to escape. That was an act, if not of faith, at least of bravery. She took a real chance, and if caught she would have been summarily executed along with the spies.*

1: That was quite a bold act, wasn't it? I wonder what impelled her to do it?

2: *A good question. Something changed her from being a person who merely dreamed about God to becoming one who acted for God. She became a key figure in God's plan.*

1: So what moved her? God?

2: *Indirectly, yes. But I think that she was initially moved by the spies themselves.*

1: In what way?

2: *Well, again I have to use a bit of imagination as I picture the scene. But I have a feeling that, for the first time, Rahab realized that she was being seen as a real person.*

1: What do you mean?

2: *The recorded conversation of Rahab with the spies includes some references to the Red Sea crossing by the Israelites. There's no way that Rahab would attribute that event to God's direct intervention unless she had been told about it by the spies. Obviously, they took the time to talk with her in some depth about God, and perhaps about other things as well. They may well have been the first people in years who saw Rahab not as a thing to be used, but as a person with whom to communicate. Perhaps they were the first persons in her memory to accept her as a human being.*

1: Oh, I see what you're saying. That's what God does: he accepts us and sees us as real. By doing that same thing, the spies were acting for God.

2: *Exactly! God reveals himself to us most frequently, it seems to me, through other people. The Israelite spies, by showing something of God's nature in their own lives, were able to help Rahab not only understand a bit of God's love, but also to respond to it.*

1: I guess I get that message. Our call is to do the same. Part of our response to God at Christmas — and at any other time — should be to share his love and his concern for others. We're to be his agents of reconciliation. As we love and accept others in the name of Christ, we can assist those persons to know and be responsive to the loving and accepting God.

2: *Right you are. Not that it's always easy to do. We are often much more ready to categorize people than to communicate with them. When the spies saw Rahab as a person, rather than just "some harlot," they had taken a giant step in assisting her to respond to God. Too often we don't take that step!*

1: Well, anyhow, they did, and they helped God's dream for Rahab became a reality. I guess God's dream for all of us is the same — that we might accept his love, accept his forgiveness, accept ourselves, and be thereby empowered to act out our faith as new persons.

2: *It's his dream, all right, and more; it's his will!*

1: Is there anything else to say?

2: *As a matter of fact, there is one final point. Do you remember how it was that Rahab and her family were spared when the Israelites finally did capture the city?*

1: Oh, sure. She had a prearranged signal with the Israelites. She placed a scarlet cord on the window of her house, and gathered her parents and brothers and sisters with her there. The cord was to be a sign to the invaders that no harm should befall those gathered in that place. It was almost like the sign of passover.

2: *I was thinking in terms of another symbol. I pictured it almost like the cross!*

1: Oh? How do you make that connection?

2: *After the city was conquered by the Israelites, Rahab and family were taken outside the camp.*

1: What does that mean?

2: *Some folks think that it is an act with particular significance. The camp of Israel would be considered holy. Unclean persons would not be allowed to enter. Perhaps Rahab's occupation placed her outside the camp.*

1: But I thought that she became a respectable citizen?

2: *She did. But perhaps a prescribed ritual for forgiveness was required before she could be considered "clean" and be permitted to dwell in the city. In any case she did eventually return to the city. She married, had children, and — as we know — became a part of the genealogy of Jesus Christ.*

1: I'm still not quite certain that I see what you're driving at. I thought we were talking about the scarlet cord, and how it might be like the cross.

2: *We are. The scarlet cord was the symbol that she trusted. And, through it, or because of it, she was spared, eventually forgiven and enabled to lead a new life. She was restored, and it wouldn't have happened without that scarlet cord!*

1: I get it. It's like our recognition that the cross is a symbol of forgiveness and restoration to us. Through it we are brought to new life, and our sins are covered by Christ.

2: *Right! The cord was Rahab's symbol of salvation; the cross is ours. Both of them serve as the means by which God's dreams become real in us. Both are signs of forgiveness.*

1: Maybe the color of that cord is significant, then. After all, it was Christ's shed blood that made salvation real for you and me.

2: *Good point! In any case, the message is clear. God loves us, and reaches out toward us in our sin to make us new. If we take seriously what God has done through the cross of Christ [which always casts its shadow over the manger] we discover that forgiveness is offered to us all. His dream is simply that we believe that, and accept it.*

1: I guess that really is a part of the Christmas story, too.

2: *Right. In fact, when we do the "hanging of the greens" in our decorating for the season, we ought — figuratively, at least — to hang a scarlet cord as well.*

1: What you're saying is that the cross ought to be as much a part of our Christmas as the manger, or the Magi, or the star of Bethlehem.

2: *Yes, because the cross is what makes the dreams of Christmas real. The dreams are God's. He loves us; his dream for us is that we respond to that love and love one another.*

1: Amen!

A DIALOGUE FOR
THE THIRD SUNDAY IN ADVENT
GOD'S LOVE
RUTH

First Reader (1): Well, we finally found an ancestor of Jesus who's worthy of the name!

Second Reader (2): I suppose that you're talking about Ruth when you say that?

1: Right! After those dialogues about Isaac, who was basically drab and colorless, and Rahab, who was — to put it delicately — promiscuous, it should be a joy to talk about Ruth! Not that we didn't learn something from Isaac and Rahab; Ruth just seems so much nicer. She was a good person; just what we'd expect for inclusion on a list of Jesus' forebears.

2: You remember her story, then?

1: Well, uh, not all of it. But I do recall something about Ruth gleaning in the fields, and I've seen the picture of that event in a dozen different churches. And I also remember that great line of Ruth's: "Whither thou goest, I will go." My recollection of the book of Ruth is simply that it is a pleasant little story. And Ruth was a pleasant person.

2: As a matter of fact, she was — but her story has some rather astounding implications for us. It's much more than a nice little tale.

1: That may be, but I seem to remember it as a tranquil interlude in the Old Testament books. Isn't it set in the middle of books about fighting and bloodshed?

2: *It is, indeed. The Book of Ruth is placed between Judges and First Samuel, which makes it an island of peace floating amidst lust, cruelty, vengeance, and warfare. Nevertheless, it has some rather strong statements to make. It may be downright revolutionary!*

1: That you'll have to show me! How about refreshing my memory? Ruth was obviously the heroine, since the book bears her name. Who were the villains in the story? What was the plot?

2: *Strangely enough, there were no villains, which makes this book unique in the Old Testament. And the story is deceptively simple, though the customs portrayed are more than a little strange.*

1: O.K. Let's hear the story.

2: *It begins with Naomi and Elimelech, a husband and wife from Bethlehem, journeying to the land of Moab due to a famine in their own country. They take their two sons with them, and during their stay in Moab, both sons marry women of that land. Unfortunately tragedy strikes and Elimelech, as well as both sons, dies. Naomi is left alone.*

1: Sounds like a feminine version of the Book of Job!

2: *If it is, Naomi at least received more comfort from Ruth than Job did from either his wife or his companions! In any case, Naomi decides to return home. One of her daughters-in-law, Ruth by name, chooses to follow Naomi back to Bethlehem. She announces her intent to Naomi in the famous words, "Whither thou goest, I will go; and where thou lodgest, I will lodge; thy people shall be my people, and thy God my God . . ."*

1: As I recall, though, things weren't much better in Israel when Naomi and Ruth returned.

2: *Quite true, at least for a while. Times are difficult, and Ruth attempts to obtain food for the two of them by gleaning in the fields, that is, picking up grain which the reapers left in the fields, after harvest, for the poor.*

1: That really is all that I remember about the story. Is there any more to it?

2: *Just a bit. Ruth gleaned in the field of a landowner named Boaz. He was somewhat attracted to Ruth, and offered her his protection as well as a shower of small favors. When Naomi heard about Boaz' interest, she pointed out that he was a distant relative, and she advised Ruth to throw herself upon his legal protection as well. This Ruth did in a rather involved ritual on the threshing floor where Boaz was sleeping one night. I'm not sure that I understand all the customs involved, but Boaz contacted the next-of-kin who waived his right to the yound widow, and then Boaz himself married Ruth. They had a child, and the book ends with Naomi holding her new grandchild in her arms.*

1: So the message, I guess, is that love conquers all. Ruth loves her mother-in-law; Boaz loves Ruth; Ruth loves Boaz ... and the all live happily ever after. That hardly seems to be what you called a revolutionary document!

2: *Love does indeed conquer, but I don't think the story of Ruth is as simplistic as you make it.*

1: O.K. You tell me what it says.

2: *It begins by suggesting that* God's love goes beyond our wildest expectations.

1: How do you figure that?

2: *The message of the book suggests that the love of God goes into some rather surprising places. For example, it extends across the bounds of race.*

1: Oh, that's right. Ruth was a foreigner, wasn't she?

2: *She certainly was. The Bible constantly stresses her alien background. Again and again she's called "stranger," "foreigner," and "the Moabitess." This becomes much more significant when you stop and realize just when this book was written.*

1: What do you mean?

2: *The Book of Ruth seems to have been written down long after its recorded events. Its composition took place at a time when the Israelite prophets were not only speaking out against foreign marriages, but were actually calling for any Jews married to foreigners to divorce them at once!*

1: Well, I'll agree that that does make the book somewhat daring — suggesting as it does that a foreign wife was a beautiful, loving person . . .

2: *. . . and also an ancestor of King David! Don't forget that!*

1: I guess that's right. The message must have been a bit upsetting to the religious leaders. How come they were so opposed to Jews marrying foreigners anyway?

2: *Well, it wasn't just that they were heartless! They really did feel that there was a rationale for their point of view. The Jews had just returned to their homeland from exile. The feeling of the prophets was that it was essential that the Jews begin to recapture their uniqueness as God's people. If they married foreign wives, they might take up foreign customs [and maybe even foreign gods]. In any case, consorting with those of different background and faith could make it easy for the Jews to lose sight of their own identity as a separate people. They were, therefore, called to keep themselves religiously and racially pure. As an aid in the process, they were asked to remember the golden years of Israel under David and Solomon.*

1: Wow! The Book of Ruth must have caused a stir at that, by not only glorifying a foreign wife, but pointing out that she was one of David's ancestors. Israel's greatest king, God's anointed leader, had mixed blood!

2: *Exactly! The author didn't preach, debate, argue, or scold. He simply told a story about a foreign wife whose devotion to her mother-in-law was as touching as it was unusual, and who ultimately became a part of God's people, in the line of the covenant. Foreign blood flowed in David's veins — and apparently that was all right with God; he still called David to be King!*

1: Maybe people could accept Ruth as a part of David's ancestry since she was such an exceptional person. She was full of love and concern, and, of course, she was beautiful. Maybe folks thought that David's comeliness came from her; that would make them more accepting of Ruth, and less likely to take the book as a polemic tract.

2: *What makes you think Ruth was beautiful?*

1: Why, everyone knows that. The Bible describes her as . . .

2: *In point of fact, the Bible never describes her at all!*

1: Really? I was sure that I read about her beauty.

2: *You just think that you did. We always assume that Ruth was beautiful, but the only thing described in the book is her character — her willingness to carry out the menial and demanding task of gleaning in fields — her willingness to give herself in marriage to a man who was probably much older, but whose kindness and concern were more important than age.*

1: I have a feeling that there's a sermon somewhere in all that!

2: *Not really a sermon, and only a secondary message from the book. But it is a good point to remember: beauty is not really a matter of what one looks like, but of who one is. When we speak of "beautiful persons" today, we're more inclined to mean someone who is loving and caring than someone who is physically attractive.*

1: I read once that God makes the unlovely lovely by loving them.

2: *I like that! And it's true. I don't know whether or not Ruth was unlovely or not to start with. But she certainly became lovely in the eyes of those around her as she demonstrated her own care and concern. Her ability to do that — to care and to love — was nothing less than a gift from God. As she was loved by God, she was able to love others.*

1: Well, if that's only the secondary message from Ruth, what's the primary one?

2: *It ought to be obvious by now. God's love goes beyond all barriers — barriers of race, nationality, economics, status — whatever. God's love, expressed through his people, is meant to reach out toward a society that is called to inclusiveness and openness, rather than to segregation and separation.*

1: And we're to love beyond all barriers, too? We're to be the vehicles through which God's love can be expressed?

2: *Right. The message is simple: Love one another without reservation! If God's love is beyond expectations — reaching out to foes as well as friends — across borders, boundaries, and all other divisions, then we, as God's people, should love with that same inclusiveness.*

1: Ruth, apparently, was able to do just that. She had a love without reservation, and — I guess — beyond expectation.

2: *She certainly did! You may remember from the story that Naomi's other daughter-in-law, Orpah by name, made all the right gestures of love. She offered to go back to Israel with Naomi; she accompanied her mother-in-law to the border; she was obedient when Naomi told her to return to her own home. Ruth went beyond the gestures, however. She had the imagination and courage to act out her love — moving to a new country, starting life anew — just because she felt that Naomi needed her. She loved without reservation.*

1: She did, indeed, and she used those beautiful words, "Whither thou goest, I will go."

2: *You know, it's interesting that you should mention those words.*

1: Why?

2: *Well, they are sometimes quoted at weddings. Not too long ago they formed the basis of a popular love song. Originally, however, they were spoken not as endearments between lovers, but as a pledge to a mother-in-law!*

1: I guess we've heard lots of mother-in-law jokes down through the years, but I doubt if Naomi was your typical mother-in-law!

2: *I wonder! The common thread in all in-law jokes is the state of tension that exists when two generations and two families never completely bridge the gaps between them.*

1: That's true, but we don't see any evidence of gaps between Naomi and Ruth. In fact, it's just the reverse. Both women are concerned for the other's welfare.

2: *Well, think about the scene where Naomi and Ruth returned to Bethlehem. Naomi's first words were, "Don't call me Naomi, but Mara [which means bitter] because God has dealt bitterly with me." There's no word there of appreciation for the daughter-in-law who followed her back to a strange land. Then she went on to say, "The Lord has brought me back empty," with still, apparently, no thought of Ruth whose very presence marks that statement as untrue.*

1: Oh, I see what you mean. Maybe Naomi wasn't so easy to live with at that.

2: *That's the way I see it, anyway. But, my point is, Ruth loved beyond the normal expectation of love. And it's interesting that the most famous and beautiful line about human love in the Bible — with the possible exception of some passages from Song of Solomon — deals with love between in-laws. The kind of relationship that we sometimes find difficult, and about which we make jokes, is held up by the Bible as model!*

1: So our call is to love our in-laws?

2: *Well, of course, we're called to do that. But that's not the basic message of Ruth. The message is that God loves across all possible barriers, and that his people are called to respond to him by loving the same way. Our call is to love the unlovely, to love our enemies, and to love one another without reservation.*

1: What does "love" really mean in that kind of context?

2: *It seems to me that it must mean more than "liking" someone. It means knowing the needs of persons, and responding to them. Maybe the need is for food, and maybe it is for understanding. Perhaps it is for assistance in self-development, and perhaps it is simply for companionship. In any case, love is a response to the needs of others.*

1: O.K., our call is to love — and this means to share our resources and ourselves with others. It means knowing enough to care, and caring enough to share. Intellectually, I'll buy that. Practically, I'm not so sure. I don't think I could possibly have the capacity to love like that. I certainly don't think I can express Christian love to people I'm not sure I really like.

2: *Your honesty, at least, is refreshing. And I'm sure that you speak for a great number of others. But there is one final thing from Ruth's story that, at least gives a hint as to a resource that may enable us to love.*

1: What's that?

2: *Do you remember the ending of the Book of Ruth?*

1: Well, I believe that you said that Ruth and Boaz married and had a child.

2: *Right, and the book ended with Naomi holding the child in her arms — no longer a bitter old woman, but a woman full of great joy because of Ruth's child.*

1: Ah, I know what you're going to say! Naomi, who had lived with tragedy piled upon tragedy, who had known poverty and resentment, whose God must have seemed either far away or silent or both for long periods of time — this woman is changed by the birth of a child. Just as we can be changed by a child!

2: *Exactly! And don't forget the locale of that birth.*

1: Oh, right. It was Bethlehem!

2: *Now, we shouldn't make an allegory out of the story. The ending of the Book of Ruth may be more an expression of grandmotherly pride than a hidden theological statement. Nevertheless, it is suggestive. A child born in Bethlehem changes our lives, brings us joy, and makes our lives new.*

1: The child toward whose birth this season points is the one who brings us power to love!

2: *Right! We're told that we can love because God first loved us. Christmas marks the reality of that love in a vivid and direct way — the season of God's coming into his world in human form to live among us to demonstrate what love is like . . .*

1: . . . and then to die for us to grant us forgiveness as well as power to live lives of love.

2: *You've got it! That says it all.*

1: It seems like a long jump from the Book of Ruth, but I guess it's not so far at that.

2: *Not at all. Ruth showed, in her life, something of the depth of love as it is meant for us all. Then, through her love and her child, another person was transformed from despair to hope — from bitterness to joy.*

1: And that other Child of Bethlehem, Jesus, offers us the same transformation, the same power to love, the same joy. He offers it not just to you and me, but to the whole world.

2: *As one of the carols of the season says, "Joy to the world; the Lord is come!"*

1: Amen!

A DIALOGUE FOR
THE FOURTH SUNDAY IN ADVENT
GOD'S FORGIVENESS
DAVID

First Reader (1): I have a quiz for you this morning. Are you ready?

Second Reader [2]: I guess so. Let's hear it.

1: It's really a short one — only one question. What biblical character am I describing? Here are the clues: He was born in Bethlehem when the fullness of time had come . . .

2: Oh, that's too easy. I know it already, it's . . .

1: Wait a minute. I want you to listen to all the clues before you answer. Here are the rest of them:
His parents were humble folk from the working class, yet he would become a king of kings.
He spent his boyhood in the Judean hills, eyes wide open to the beauty of the world around him — lilies of the fields, fleecy sheep — yet he was destined to be a great leader rather than a poetic dreamer.
His parents would misunderstand his mission, but he became God's anointed.
Palm branches would be waved before him at Jerusalem, yet many followers would forsake him at his death.
One author would report his last words as, "Into thy hands I render up my spirit."
Now — who is it?

2: Well, that's so obviously Jesus Christ that I suspect a trick! Therefore, I'll say . . . David!

52

1: Ah, you guessed it . . . and you're right! Uncanny, isn't it? The parallels really boggle the mind, although I must admit that the quotation about David's last words came from a contemporary novelist rather than a biblical source.* Nevertheless, the other events of David's life suggest a close identification with the life of Christ.

2: *I suppose that's not really too surprising at that. Jesus is called the Son of David throughout the Gospels. The whole point of Matthew's genealogy in the first place was to show that Jesus' ancestry could be traced back to King David.*

1: All of which serves as a pretty good introduction to the subject of today's conversation.

2: *So today we talk about David? It's hard to know where to begin. There's so much material about him in the books of Samuel and Chronicles that our dialogue could go on for hours!*

1: So it could. We could talk about David and Goliath, or David and Jonathan . . .

2: *Or David and Bathsheba!*

1: I might have known that you'd pick that one! But you have a point. We're usually much more interested in discussing other people's sins than their virtues. The Bathsheba incident certainly shows David at his very worst.

2: *Does it ever! Coveting, adultery, murder are just three of the aspects of that particular episode.*

1: You're right. And, I suppose that we do need to have some understanding of sin if we are to appropriately

---

* *David the King* — Gladys Schmitt

prepare for the coming of a Savior. So the Bathsheba story is a good place to start. We don't need to go into all the details, though. It's a pretty familiar story.

2: *Probably so, but we ought to at least outline it to set the stage for discussion.*

1: Why don't you do that? You're the one who brought it up.

2: *Well, King David was attracted by the charms of a woman named Bathsheba, and felt that he must have her for himself. That she was already married to one of his captains named Uriah was a complication, but not a major one for a monarch. He did, indeed, take Bathsheba, and then sent word to his field commander that Uriah was to be put in the front ranks of battle. At a given signal the soldiers nearby would withdraw, leaving Uriah exposed to the enemy. The orders were carried out and Uriah was slain by the enemy, but David was just as guilty of that death as if he had hurled the Ammonite spear that slew him.*

1: I guess those are the major details of the story. Even in that brief version we have a graphic description of David's sin.

2: *We do, indeed, but what does it really have to say to us today? Particularly at Christmas?*

1: Maybe the most important thing about the story is that it appears at all! In an age of doctored tapes, presidential coverups, and public relations image-making, we may find ourselves astonished that the biblical writers in portraying Israel's greatest king for posterity should show him with all his shortcomings. It was almost as if they were deliberately setting out to say sin is a reality. It strikes at us all, even the ruler of Israel's golden era, and the compiler of the majestic psalms of praise and thanksgiving. That being the case, sin probably won't miss you and me.

2: *I suppose that could be part of the message, but I wonder how helpful it really is. Sure, misery loves company, and I'm glad to know that in my sin I'm in some pretty good company. But isn't the story of David and Bathsheba simply a chance for me to rationalize my own conduct? If sin is all right for David, it must be all right for me, too.*

1: I'm not quite sure what you mean by "being all right." Nothing in David's story makes sin all right. In fact, we get a pretty realistic look at some of sin's results, and they don't make for pleasant reading.

2: *What is the point of the story?*

2: Certainly one aspect of it is the fact that the *results of sin can be permanent.*

2: *They were certainly permanent for Uriah!*

1: Precisely my point. Sin's consequences can leave a great many scars that never go away, even if repentance eventually comes about.

2: *I'm sure that's true, but let's face it: I'm not ever going to have someone murdered as David did.*

1: Of course you won't. Or, at least, I hope not. But your sins and mine may differ from David's only in degree.

2: *What do you mean?*

1: Like David, we frequently act on our own self-centered impulses. We put our own appetities and desires before anything or anyone else. We use other people, and I'm not simply speaking in sexual terms. We use people whenever we manipulate them, when we refuse to let them be themselves, when we seek to work our will on them even if it is — as we so often rationalize — "for their own good."

2: *Well, when you put it that way, I suppose that I have used people from time to time. And nations and classes of people have done the same thing to other nations and other classes.*

1: Right. And there's another aspect of sin that concerns me.

2: *What's that?*

1: It's the tendency of our individual sin to affect those that are closest to us. It often has a permanent affect on our own families, to say nothing of the mark it leaves on ourselves.

2: *Does the David and Bathsheba story say that?*

1: Not in so many words, but the events that surround it proclaim it loud and clear. I think that there are a number of passages which indicate that David really did care about his family. Certainly his apparent over-indulgence with his children points toward a need on his part to feel their love. His tears at the death of the son who had led an armed revolt against him speaks of a longing for love even then.

2: *You're not suggesting that David's involvement with Bathsheba ultimately affected his whole family? That it might finally have resulted in his own son's rebellion against him?*

1: I wonder! From all that we read, David was a nearly faultless field commander. As a general, he inspired fanatical loyalty on the part of his troops. Yet his own home was quite different. It turned out to be a place of incest, murder, and revolt. And, yes, maybe that rebellion on the part of Absalom happened because David had not been able to be the kind of father that was needed. Perhaps his own inner struggles, his own awareness of guilt, made it impossible for David to offer fatherly counsel and guidance when most needed. His own sin affected all of his relationships — particularly with those who knew him best. Sin always seems to do that; it makes us unable to relate to others as we were created to relate.

2: *You may be right. However, this sermon seems to be getting less and less "Christmasy." I thought that a dialogue about David would lead us to a consideration of royalty, helping us focus our attention on the King of Kings who came to us on that first Christmas. Instead, my off-hand comment about David and Bathsheba has gotten us all tied up in the most unpleasant side of David's nature. Can't we move in another direction?*

1: I'm glad that you put it that way. Because that is precisely the message of Christmas.

2: *I don't get it. What's the message?*

1: That we can more in another direction.

2: *Oh.*

1: I saw a sermon title on a bulletin board once that said, "CHRISTMAS IS FOR GIVING." I didn't hear the sermon, but I had a feeling that the title may have said it all. What a great one! It's mean to be a pun, I'm sure, indicating that Christmas is a time for *giving*, but also a time of *forgiving*. Forgiveness, of course, is what Christmas is all about.

2: *What's the connection with David in all of this?*

1: It seems to me that David may well be the classic example of a sinful person who was called by God . . . and then changed by God. It was God's forgiveness that enabled David to be the person he was created to be.

2: *How do you know all that from the stories of David?*

1: I think it can be inferred from what we know about David. We don't know, of course, how many of the psalms were written by David . . .

2: *As a matter of fact, we don't know for sure if any of them were really written by David, do we?*

1: No, we aren't absolutely sure of that. But we do know that many of the psalms included in the Book of Psalms in our Old Testament were attributed to David. At the very least, he must have collected them, prayed them, and sung them.

2: *Probably so, but what does that have to do with what we were talking about?*

1: Simply that the overwhelming message of the psalms is of the importance of a relationship with God — a God who knows and cares for individuals (and nations) despite their rebellion and shortcomings, and who continues to draw them to himself. I don't think David would have been able to sing — much less compose — any psalms unless he had experienced God's forgiveness and acceptance. They would have been too much a mockery for him.

2: *You may have a point there. In any case, the stories of David indicate that he did, indeed, feel the presence of God again and again.*

1: Right. And, as a matter of fact, we discover passages indicating David and God had a meaningful relationship both before and after his involvement with Bathsheba. As a shepherd lad in the fields and as a young man facing Goliath, he was secure in his understanding of God's presence with him. But years later, as commander in the field and as king of Israel, he was equally assured of the power and the presence of the living God.

2: *Hey! That's neat! That says that even after he turned away from God — caught up in his own self-centeredness and destroying those who stood in his way — God still reached out to him in love.*

1: Exactly. God changed him back into what he was meant to be. Did you ever hear that song "Yesterday"?

2: *I'm not sure that I did.*

1: Well, I don't remember much more of it than one line, but I've always liked that line: "I believe in yesterday." I think that God believes in yesterday, too.

2: *What do you mean?*

1: God believes in the innocence and wonder of childhood — and restores us to it through forgiveness. Oh, life can never be what it once was, once we are caught up by sin. Nevertheless, God can restore our relationship with him; God can offer us a new beginning. In that sense, he gives us back our yesterday. That's the real message of Christmas.

2: *And if we stumble again — he offers forgiveness again?*

1: I think that's the gospel. And that's what David discovered. I have a feeling that the reason David is remembered as Israel's greatest king is not simply because he extended the borders, established new trade routes, stabilized the kingdom, and consolidated the government, nor even because he was able to compile the Psalter for coming generations to use in worship and praise. He is remembered because he was a person who walked with God, even *after* he had been caught up in the most gross of sins. Like you and me, he was self-centered and hurt those around him. Yet God loved him, forgave him, and gave him power to become new. David is remembered because he stands for what all of us can still become — forgiven sinners, beginning life all over.

2: *That is a Christmas message, after all. God's gift to David, and to us, is forgiveness and the opportunity of new life.*

1: Of course. We look toward that manger in the City of David, and are aware that the reason for God's coming to the world in a little child is so that we would be able to see in his life the meaning of forgiveness. It's no accident that the Child of Bethlehem ultimately becomes the man on the cross, whose final words are those of forgiveness for people who may not even be aware of their sin.

2: *So Christmas, as you said earlier, is for giving and for forgiveness. Rod McKuen said it differently in one of his poems. He said that Christmas is just another word for love.*

1: That's not very different at all! For the Christmas message is that love and forgiveness are all intertwined. Together they represent the gift of God to humankind.

2: *And David's life exemplified what ours can be if we believe that — changed through the presence of God.*

1: Yes, indeed. Perhaps we ought to be as happy as kings, not just because — as Robert Louis Stevenson tells us — "the world is so full of a number of things", but because the world is full of the presence of God. His forgiveness, through Jesus Christ, is a gift to be received with joy!

2: *Amen.*

A DIALOGUE FOR CHIRSTMAS
GOD'S GIFT
JOSEPH

[AUTHOR'S NOTE: Although this sermon involves two persons, it is not a dialogue as are the others in the book. It is really a monologue by Joseph, with the narrator used to set the scene. It would be appropriate for use on Christmas Eve, or on Christmas Day, as a special program itself, or as a part of a service of worship.]

Narrator: Joseph shivered for a moment, and drew his cloak around his shoulders. The desert was a cold place at night; who would have guessed it during the oppressive heat of the day, with the sun scorching the sand. For a moment he looked longingly at the camp fire behind him. He almost turned back, but just then a raucous laugh burst forth and he went on. "Not tonight," he said to himself. "I just can't take any more tonight. I've had enough cynicism, enough curses, enough blasphemy, enough stories about runaway camels to last a lifetime!"

Even as he said it, he managed a rueful smile. That was hardly a fair picture of those men back by the fire. They weren't really bad folks, and they certainly had been gracious to allow his wife and child to accompany them on the caravan. They were just typical camel drivers — bored with constant trips back and forth between Israel and Egypt. Cynics they might have been — they'd seen enough bargaining in the eastern cities to assume that everyone had his price — but at heart they were probably good men. They simply filled the evening hours with the crude stories with little or no meaning that are found in barracks, camps, marketplaces, or wherever men gather together with time on their hands.

They were probably family men, too, and they must have missed their wives and children.

Instinctively, Joseph looked over to where Mary and the child lay sleeping, shielded by a bush and pile of stones from the evening winds. No sign of restlessness there, and Joseph walked on.

"I ought to go back and lie down with them," he thought. "Those drivers will be up at the crack of dawn. But somehow I don't feel sleepy. Heaven knows, I ought to be. When have I really slept in these past few days?"

His thoughts were interrupted by a sudden shout from the camp fire area: "Hey, Pharaoh, don't get lost in the desert! You'll never get a pyramid until you sit on a thorn for a while!" The others in the circle were probably collapsing with mirth at that wit; Joseph waved a hand and moved on.

"Pharaoh, indeed," he thought, but it was his own fault, and he knew it. He never should have told them about the dream. The minute he first mentioned the dream, one of the drivers had cried out, "Here's another Joseph going down to Egypt who hears God in his dreams! The last one became a king; this one's bound to be a pharoah! Maybe his coat isn't so colorful as the one we used to hear stories about, but his dreams have more class." And, of course, they had called him "Pharaoh" ever since.

"Ever since." It had been only four days that they were on the road, but it felt almost like an eternity — particularly now that they had pushed into the interior of this strange land of Egypt, with its unbroken horizon of barren sand. Cairo was still a good week's journey away; he felt as if he was passing through an unknown world. He wondered what it would be like to live in an Egyptian city. How could he ever live apart from the Galilean hills where he had spent all of his life up until now. Could pyramids ever replace the mountains for Mary?

Engrossed in thought, Joseph hardly noticed where he was walking when suddenly a shadow loomed up before him. Now, Joseph was a tall muscular man; his strength such that more than once he had put his shoulder under a Roman axle and lifted a broken chariot from the mire. On unfamiliar ground, however, in a world that seemed completely different from all that he had known, he gave a quick cry of surprise, threw up his hands, and ducked his head.

Then, to his amazement, the shadow snorted; it was a whimsical and musical sound that he had come to know well these past four days, and Joseph laughed aloud. He had wandered over to the area where the camels were tethered, and had all but knocked over old Balaam, the camel on which Mary and the child had been riding each day. Joseph had never been close to camels before this hurried flight from his native land, but he put out his hand with the sure touch of one who is at home with animals. The calloused palm rubbed old Balaam's neck, just as it had rubbed the necks of countless oxen while he shaped yokes for them. Joseph had been proud of his carpentry, and it was his boast — never refuted by anyone — that no animal would feel uncomfortable wearing one of his yokes.

Balaam, of course, wore no yoke — only the harness befitting the "ship of the desert" as the drivers liked to call their camels. And they were graceful animals, at that. Even with their huge humps, thick callosities on their chests and leg joints, and broad sole pad on their feet, they had a regal bearing. They probably would have considered themselves vastly superior to the common beasts of burden with which Joseph was so familiar.

But an animal was an animal, and a friendly touch was a friendly touch, and Balaam stood still under the friendly pat of the strong hand. The beast curved its neck back as far as it could, so that it almost appeared to be looking Joseph in the eye.

"I wonder what she sees," Joseph thought. "A foolish old man?" Balaam peered with unblinking eyes and comprehending stare, and suddenly Joseph felt a rush of words welling up within him. After all, talking to a camel was better than talking to himself. It was even hard to talk with Mary now, caught up as she was in the miracle of motherhood. As he had already discovered in conversation with the camel drivers, no one else could remotely understand all the events of the recent past. But he had to say something to someone.

Joseph took a deep breath. Behind him the fire flickered and then flared up again. The wind whistled briefly. Joseph ruffled the hair on the neck of the camel, and began to speak.

Joseph: Well, Balaam, it's this way. A few months ago, I was just another carpenter in Nazareth. No, that's not quite true. I wasn't just any other carpenter — I was the carpenter — the one who was betrothed to the most wonderful girl in the world!

It was Mary. She was going to marry me. Why she chose me over the younger, more handsome, more charming men of the village, I'll never know. She even laughed when her friends said, "He'll make a yoke for you like he makes for everyone else's oxen, and you'll end up ploughing the fields!"

O, Balaam, you can't imagine how I felt in those days. I can't begin to describe it. But, then, one day, it happened. I still remember it; Mary had been acting somewhat strangely . . . but I had supposed that all women have such moments as they approach wedding time. I guess also that in the back of my mind was the feeling that she might decide that it was all a mistake — that she wanted to marry one of the younger men. I knew that I wasn't really good enough for her.

But on this day she met me at her door and said, "Joseph, we must talk." Well, Balaam, it was almost as if I had played that scene before. I was sure that she was about to say, "I can't go through with the wedding; I'm not sure . . ." or, "I'm too young," or some such thing. I was utterly unprepared, however, for what she did say.

It wasn't much; she just said, quietly, "Joseph, I'm with child!"

One time I had been fashioning a chest for a man, and had it on my workbench using a chisel on the legs. Suddenly the leg of the bench buckled, and the chest fell on top of me. I can still remember my initial feeling of utter surprise [which shouldn't have been there at all, for the leg had been wobbly and I knew it], and the wave of nausea that hit me as the pain crashed into my chest. Somehow, I felt exactly the same way as Mary spoke. I couldn't believe it. And she said it so calmly. My little Mary, whose purity had seemed to engulf her very life, pregnant! And then her words virtually tumbled out — how it was not by a man, but by God's spirit, that she was with child — and how that child would be . . . the Messiah!

Well, Balaam, if there was another word beside purity that I had always associated with Mary, it was wisdom. I know that most folks these days think that wisdom is reserved for the elders, not young girls. But Mary was a person with whom you could talk. She could converse about Roman law and Philistine culture; she had a curiosity about everything, and a mind that was sharp. [Much more so than mine, as a matter of fact!] But in one moment, that whole concept exploded. Her incoherent ramblings about God's spirit made her appear addled and confused. Could it have been the Galilean sun, or maybe just the shock of the impending marriage to an old carpenter? I didn't know. But something disastrous had happened. Her purity and her wisdom were gone in one fell swoop. And I was sick.

I looked at her, still captivated by her beauty [that beauty which she wore as carelessly as if it were an old shawl], thought for a brief moment of what might have been, and then — without a word — turned on my heel and walked away. I couldn't trust myself to speak.

I'd planned to do it quietly, when I was able to put some rational thoughts together. I would put her away, quietly arranging the divorce so that there would be no shame. Whether that was planned for compassion for Mary, or to protect my own pride, I don't know. I wanted no public demonstration, however. She could have been stoned, of course. Adultery is adultery, whether during the period of betrothal or after the marriage itself. But I could not let that happen. And I lay down, in a stupor, and slept.

And then it happened! The dream that was as vivid as anything that ever happened in my life. I heard a voice, and I saw someone . . . or something, I never could be quite sure . . . but the voice was as real as that hump of yours, Balaam! It said that I should not fear to take Mary as my wife, that the child within her was indeed a child of God's Spirit, and that the child was to be called Jesus, for he would save his people from their sins.

I've never been much of a man for dreams; but this was reality. This was as real as anything in my world. I don't begin to understand it, Balaam, but I believed it. In some mysterious fashion that a poor carpenter like me can never find the words to explain, God had come upon Mary to produce within her a son who would be a savior of us all.

And that was important — far more so than my instant realization that I could marry Mary after all, that she was neither impure nor mad. God was doing something here, and I had to take it seriously even though I couldn't understand it.

Maybe that's the first thing we all have to learn about God, Balaam, that we must take him seriously, we must trust him, even though we may never completely understand him. He's God, not one of us, and his ways are strange, so all we can do is trust. We can't explain God, anymore than you can explain how you store up water in that stomach of yours for a long trip — but the water's there when you need it, isn't it? And God's here, too. I don't have to understand him completely, Balaam. I just have to take him seriously. And that's what I did.

Narrator: Joseph stopped. It was quite still. The wind had died down; there were no sounds from the campfire area. Apparently the drivers had settled down for the night. Balaam stretched his graceful neck, and turned back toward the other camels. Joseph broke the silence.

Joseph: That's not the end of the story, Balaam. Not at all. What happened next was just as strange, and just as wonderful. We were married, and the world became a beautiful place once more. Together Mary and I began to experience that miracle of growth. She became large, and we could feel the first kicking signs of life of our unborn child. [I call him "ours" even though he wasn't really mine.] Somehow, God's spirit seemed to include me in the blessing. His gift was life; it was a time of joy.

And then once more a shattering blow came. Not as bad as the other, of course, but still a difficult thing to bear. It was a royal decree. A new tax was to be imposed, and along with it a new registration. Each of us had to go to his own city. Ours was the city of David — Bethlehem. The trip to Bethlehem would normally have been neither long nor difficult. But Mary was ready to give birth at any moment. To go up and down those hills would be an exceedingly difficult journey for an expectant mother. All I could think, when I heard of the order, was, "What if we lose the baby? What if God's Messiah perishes because of some idiotic decree that all adults have to take a trip?"

I suppose that my faith and trust in God was less than complete, because we didn't lose the baby at all. I tried for an exemption — to see if Mary might be released from the necessity of the trip — but I should have saved my breath. The Roman official was sympathetic, but could do nothing. "There are no exceptions to the decree," he responded to my every query. So off we went to Bethlehem. And the baby was born.

Born in a stable, Balaam. What do you think of that? For, you see, there simply wasn't any room in any of the caravansaries in Bethlehem. We were lucky to find room in the stable yard of one of the old inns. And there, in the stable, Mary brought forth her child. We called him "Jesus."

But then a strange thing happened. Almost as soon as she gave birth, there came a rattling of the latch on the stable door, and a voice called out, "Is there a baby in there?"

Well, what do you answer to a question like that? What was going to happen? Who was calling? Would harm come to the child? I could hear murmurings from outside. There was more than one person there. I didn't really know what to do, and I was frightened — though I'm a man rarely frightened by anything. I reached for my staff, and said, "Why?"

Just then the little child let out a faint cry; someone outside said, "That's it," and before I knew what had happened the door burst open and they all crowded into the barn.

I could see in a moment that these men were bent on no harm — and they obviously sensed a presence in the stable. It was a presence that perhaps I had grown so used to it in the past days and months that I no longer noticed it myself. They sank to their knees, and one old man said simply, "He's come. I have seen salvation." Another old man would say somewhat the same thing later on in the temple, but somehow I was more touched by the tone and voice of the old shepherd [I soon discovered that all of the men were shepherds, and had come straight from their fields]. The old shepherd had a trace of wonder in his words, as if it were all beyond his comprehension, but so very real.

They didn't stay long; just looked at Mary and the baby and seemed satisfied then to make their way back to the fields. It was funny; there was none of the good-natured banter that I had seen on other occasions with new parents. No one shook my hand, or offered their best wishes. They seemed almost reluctant to *speak, as if a spell might be broken. But their eyes told the story; they had seen a great light — they had seen the Lord's anointed — and they knew it. The idea that I could have ever doubted God's plan made me feel awfully small at that moment.*

They weren't the only visitors we had, Balaam. There were not only peasants, but kings as well. They came on camels with more elaborate trappings than you've ever seen, though you'd look good in them, Balaam, and they brought gifts to the young child.

My cup was running over. A new son, recognition of God's actions in him by shepherds and kings alike, my wife at my side; I had everything I could want . . . and then came the other dream. As I lay beside Mary, I was conscious of a voice telling me to take her and the child and flee to Egypt. King Herod, I was told, sought the life of the child. That a king could be the least bit interested in a carpenter's offspring would have been ridiculous a month ago; by now, nothing seemed out of the question. And the dream was just as real as the other one. God was calling once more!

So I roused Mary and the child, and we started out for Egypt not at all sure how we might find our way. Then we met you and your masters and joined the caravan. These past four days I've been thinking about our flight. We've left behind us all of the life that we know. Even my carpenter's tools are back in Nazareth. I don't know what will happen in Egypt, or how we'll make a living. But I do know this: It's not enough just to believe in God. We've got to respond to him, too. And if responding means venturing out into an uncharted path, why, that's just what we've got to do. Knowing the stories about the actions of God — his workings with Abraham, Isaac, and Jacob — isn't enough. Reminiscing about the glory days of God's great King David isn't enough. We have to respond to God ourselves. We have to move out to follow him when he calls.

Narrator: Joseph stopped again, and shook his head. He had been louder than he meant to be. If those camel drivers heard him talking to a camel, he'd never hear the end of it. They'd think him a madman for sure.

No sounds from the area of the smoldering camp fire, though. Everyone was still asleep. Joseph patted old Balaam once more, and turned back toward the camp. Then he stopped, a quizzical look on his face. He spoke once more.

Joseph: You know, Balaam, I wish I knew how this would all turn out. Here I am with a new wife and a new child, coming to a new land. I trust God, but I wish I could understand his plan. What does it all really mean? Mary's son is to save his people from their sins. But how? What will he do? Will he grow up and lead troops in the field against Romans? That's what we always thought God's Messiah would do, but what does that have to do with sin? I wonder . . . I had the strangest feeling, Balaam, when I first saw the child. It was almost as if I'd seen him before! That doesn't make any sense at all, of course. And I don't even know what I mean by that. It wasn't any one physical feature — just a certain "something." I felt like saying, "Oh, it's you . . ." but I don't know who the "you" is when I look at Jesus. I'm not sure who I'm talking about . . . and I'm sure it doesn't make much sense, especially to a camel!

There used to be a proverb that the folks back in Isreal would use from time to time: "The child is father of the man." I'm not sure why it keeps running through my mind; I think that it just means something about all of us finally becoming the kinds of people we are because of the way we spend our childhood. But I just can't get it out of my mind: "The child is father of the man!"

Wait a minute! That's it! Of, course, Balaam, that's what it's all about. No wonder the child seemed familiar. It's . . . it's God himself! Somehow the child is Father of us all. In some utterly fantastic way, God himself has

*come. God is in that child. It's not just a Messiah, but
God, himself, Balaam; God himself! And because God has
come — because he's actually here — all of life is
different. I thought it was only me — me and my dreams
and my Mary — but it's for all of us. The world is a
different place, now. God's in it. He's given us the gift of
himself!*

Narrator: And so he did. God gave us our greatest
gift — the gift of himself in the person of Jesus. It was a
gift which would change the world, and would change
lives. It is a gift for us all, overcoming our sin and
empowering us to love. Believing in it, we shall not
perish, but have everlasting life.
Thanks be to God!
Amen!

EPILOGUE

The ancestry of Jesus includes a wide variety of persons. There were brave men and bland ones, pure women and promiscuous ones, kings and carpenters.

But the progeny of Jesus is just as varied. It includes all of us, saints and sinners, courageous and cowardly, women and men. We are all his children, redeemed by his grace, strengthened by his spirit. Our call is to believe, to accept, and to follow the God who has offered us himself in Christ.

It is not always an easy task, but the promise is that God is with us, and that we are, indeed, his children and
". . .if children, then heirs,
heirs of God and fellow heirs
with Christ, provided we suffer
with him in order that we
may also be glorified with him."

Romans 8:17